I made this book
to show how much
I love you!

To _ _ _ _ _ _ _ _ _ _ _ _ _

From _ _ _ _ _ _ _ _ _ _ _ _ _

My dad looks like this :

Our favorite thing to do together is

_____

_____

_____

_____

You are super awesome because you

_____

_____

_____

_____

The best thing about you is

_____

_____

_____

_____

You always smile when

_____

_____

_____

_____

Me & My Dad

A poem about my dad

You are the happiest when

_____

_____

_____

_____

You are there for me when

_____

_____

_____

_____

My favorite memory of us

_____

_____

_____

_____

_____

_____

_____

You taught me how to

_____

_____

_____

_____

We all had so much fun when we went to

I like it when you tell me that I am

_____

_____

_____

_____

You make me laugh when

_____

_____

_____

_____

The funniest thing you do is

_____

_____

_____

_____

You always help me to

_____

_____

_____

_____

You are good at

_____

_____

_____

_____

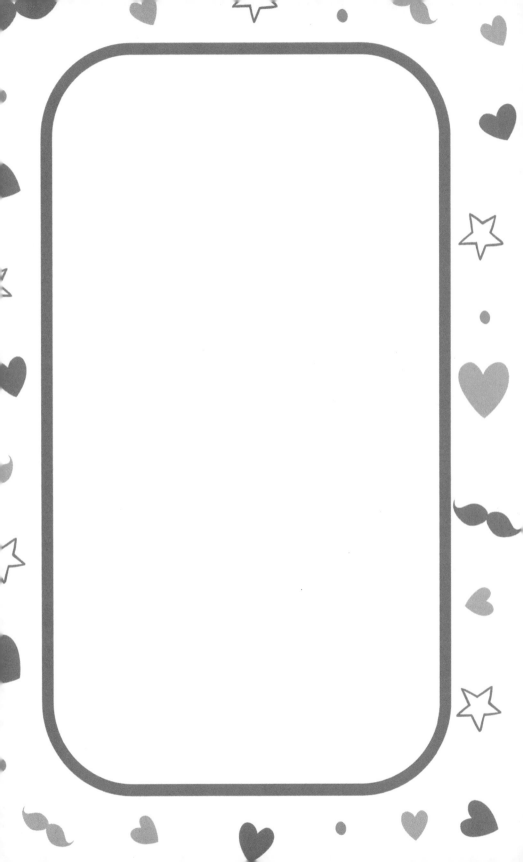

You are
smarter than

_____

_____

_____

_____

Your favorite food is

_____

_____

_____

_____

Movie/TV show that we both love is

_____

_____

_____

_____

I enjoyed a lot when we went to

_____

_____

_____

_____

I love
you
because

I'm proud to say you are

_____

_____

_____

_____

Made in United States
Troutdale, OR
06/09/2023

10524217R10030